The Jedi Code: A Jedi's True Ally?

Module One

What you feed your soul is what you harvest with your actions. -Shannon L. Alder

What is the Jedi Code?

In the Starwars Universe, the Jedi Code was a collection of rules, and guidelines, which defined what it meant to be a Jedi, and outlined the expectations placed on a member of the Jedi Order. The Jedi Code first appeared in 1987 in the first edition of the Star Wars Roleplaying game; this code was the one beginning with "There is no Emotion". This code has come to be known as the Jedi Mantra within the Jedi community, due to the structure of said code, and it was written by Greg Costikyan exclusively for the game. It was this code that was first used by the pioneers of Jedi realism and Jediism, appearing as early at the Jedi Praxeum (195) as created by Kharis Nightflyer, and this is the root of why even now most Jedi use the code five-line version of the Jedi Code (2003 version). The five-line code is a derivative of the 1987 code, with elements taken from another version of the code published in 1996: a version best known as the Yet Code.

Aside from the Jedi Mantra (five-line code), another code known in the community as the Jedi Creed (or Skywalker code), is relatively popular. Authored, and published in 1999, it was very different in structure; and instead of being presented in a mantra style, was a collection of values and statements about the purpose of the Jedi. As such, it became relatively popular among those Jedi who first came to the community after the release of Starwars Episode I. It also gained traction by making exact statements about what it means to be a Jedi, in contrast to the abstract nature of the Jedi Mantra.

The foundation of the Jedi Realist community, and Jediism, the Jedi codes have provided a guide for living for many for nearly twenty years and have been a source of transformative experiences for others. Many examples of this can be found in the text; the Jedi Compass, as well as by exploring the Jedi community at large.

Understanding the Jedi Mantra

As the original "Code" and the most widely used we shall first explore the mantra. Published prior to even the earliest Jedi groups were formed, it has been the foundational work of almost all Jedi Realist Philosophy. To understand the Mantra, it is important to understand the lexicon, or language, within the mantra. Rather than explore each line individually, due to the different versions existing, we shall explore instead the words of each Line that are Key to understanding the code regardless of general structure.

The First Line: Emotion and Peace

There is currently no scientific consensus on a definition of the word Emotion. As a word in the English language it is often used interchangeably with mood, temperament, personality, disposition, and motivation: or even as an umbrella term for all the aforementioned. We might, for practical considerations, use the following broad definition: Emotions, or an emotion, are the complex experience of consciousness, bodily sensation, and behaviour that reflects the personal significance of an object, event, or circumstance. This broad definition is very much how Jedi explore the term emotion: informative of our surroundings and our experience.

Thankfully, peace is more easily defined: in a social sense, peace means a lack of conflict (such as war) and freedom from fear of violence between individuals or groups. On an individual scale it can be used to infer freedom from disturbance: to exist in state of tranquillity. In simple terms: a period in which there is no war or a war has ended, or inner-peace, respectively.

Now, to understand how these terms intertwine, we must further explore emotion first. For the sake of simplicity, psychologists and laypeople alike often divide the experience of emotion into those that are positive and those that are negative. This, too, is present in Jedi thinking, if one looks to the fiction:

"Fear is the path to the dark side. Fear leads to anger. Anger leads to hate. Hate leads to suffering." – Yoda, Star Wars: The Empire Strikes back (George Lucas, 1983)

Here, fear is framed as an inherently "negative" emotional experience that can lead only to further emotions framed as negative. In some ways this is still true of Jedi philosophy in general, however. the complexity of emotions makes language which relies on oppositions suspect. Consider love, which is often framed as positive, yet life has taught most of us it can lead to painful and destructive outcomes. Let us reconsider fear too: it is indeed a negative feeling, that can have a debilitating effect, but it can be motivating for the person experiencing fear. In the proper context, in which one ought to be afraid, it informs the person on why they need to change the situation or do something to change the situation.

This is how we view emotion from the Jedi Perspective: is it proper for the context? An emotion is not a problem in of itself, but how it forms, and how the experience informs our actions can be. To return to the quote by Yoda: fear can lead to further emotions that might not be proper, and this is true of all emotions. I mentioned love before: love is a wonderful thing, yet, the complications of relationships can lead to a multitude of other strong emotions and many which can be problematic. That is often the difficulty with having a healthy relationship with our emotional content: we feel it and experience it. We do not will into happening the emotions we feel.

Now, let us apply the concept of peace to this understanding of emotion: the freedom from disturbance and to exist in state of tranquillity. One might interpret this to mean that the absence of emotion is the swiftest path to tranquillity: that emotion being often unpredictable and dominated by our personal bias, and reactions to external stimuli outside our control, should be subsumed by cold logic and rationality. That we should set aside our emotional content, and instead control them with rational and objective thinking. Aside from being impossible: no human is bereft of emotion, this is also misguided. A lack of empathy, and an understanding for the emotional content of a situation, are the makings of poor leadership. Similarly, it is also a barrier to successfully navigating the difficult times of interpersonal relationships.

The Jedi approach to emotion is underlined by the word peace because it reminds us of the most essential lesson of having a healthy relationship with our emotions. Do not engage in conflict with them: when you try to control emotion, you spend energy in "not feeling" and in doing so make the emotion you are trying to fight more prevalent. You become distracted by an internal conflict, and indeed, by not experiencing the emotion in the suitable context, you create a future conflict where you must deal with the incongruence of the experience. As Jedi, we accept the emotion, we listen to what it informs us about the situation, and we allow it to be. We do not engage in conflict with our emotion: we do not "other" our emotions. They are not an object separate from us: they are a part of us. We listen and ask: why am I angry? Why am I sad? We channel our emotion as a source of information from which we can intuit how others might be experiencing the situation: it helps us develop an empathetic understanding of others.

Similarly, it allows us to remain congruent with the situation, to keep ourselves present in the situation. Thus, peace is to not engage in conflict with yourself: it is to accept emotion. Emotion is just another experience that is fundamental to you: it is not inherently positive or negative, it is the context that decides that. Your emotional content does not have to become an action: anger does not need to become an angry outburst or lashing out, it could become a talking point for resolving situations and strengthening relationships.

The Second Line: Ignorance and Knowledge

Ignorance is simply a lack of knowledge or information. A text book definition of knowledge is a familiarity with someone or something, including include facts, descriptions, information, or skills acquired through experience or education. It can further refer to the theoretical or practical understanding of a subject: which can be implicit or explicit.

In the field of Epistemology; knowledge and its nature continue to be a subject of debate. Plato's famous definition was "justified true belief." However, it can be argued it is axiomatic to state that something must be believed to be known. A thought experiment can show the issues with Justified True Belief as a working model of what knowledge is. If we take an object, say a blue box, but you do not believe the box is blue, you do not have knowledge of that fact regardless of belief: belief is insufficient to claim something as knowledge.

Thus, we must consider truth: if you believe that the box is blue, and it is blue. Then, your belief is consistent with the truth, and thus you have some element of knowledge. Yet, this is still not enough. A belief may be consistent with the truth, but it may not in fact be justified: it may be mere coincidence.

Thus, knowledge must be justified. If you believe that the box is blue because you have seen the box and confirmed it is blue: then you have knowledge that is justified by empirical means. It is not an assertion which has no basis in the observed truth.

If we accept the thought experiment than ultimately knowledge has little to do with belief: it is an empirical observation of the objective reality. Yet, we should consider the distinction between "knowledge by description" and "knowledge by acquaintance" as asserted in Problems of Philosophy by Bertrand Russell. Knowledge by acquaintance is obtained through a direct empirical interaction between a person and the object that person is perceiving. To return to our thought experiment, in other words, justified true belief can only occur through direct contact with the object. It is empirical experience of the facts that is meant by knowledge by acquaintance.

This is contrasted with knowledge by description: when one is not directly acquainted with a fact but knows it only by a description, one arguably is not entirely justified in holding a proposition undeniably true. Even if the source could be considered vetted and reliable: there is an element of doubt presented by the lack of direct contact.

We should also consider the concept of Family Resemblances as proposes by Wittgenstein (1953): Things which could be thought to be connected by one common feature may in fact be connected by various similarities yet have no one feature that is common to all things. This applies directly to the use of language and description: various words have synonyms and variations. This applies also to knowledge itself: one thing might be alike to another, yet distinct, but how one relates to it and absorbs this knowledge (direct or indirect) is by contextualising it with existing knowledge: connecting the over-lapping similarities.

The range of one's own vocabulary and your use of language also frames how you experience the knowledge of others. The meanings of words are democratic: how the general populous use them is how they are used. How you perceive what you see or experience, based on your internal cognitions and emotions, will also frame your "knowledge".

As Jedi, we believe we share an objective reality, that we can all change and have a responsibility to. That the past is objective, though our memory of it might be different from others. We do believe in absolute objectivity in that we believe a situation happened as it happened: the only subjective aspect is the perspective of those involved. Consider video footage, the written word, and recorded music. We all objectively see, read, or listen to the exact same thing, yet we all remember and experience it differently.

As Jedi we thus believe in the concept of an absolute truth, however, we regard knowledge as imperfect and framed by the limitations of human experience (Sense-Data is finite), and we all have a unique experience of self. We have an internal domain which has no neighbours. Thus, we accept the burden that is ignorance, yet in turn we remember knowledge is power.

Returning to justified true belief: as Jedi we seek the justification and the truth to frame our understanding and beliefs about situations. All our knowledge may be charged to be subjective, despite coming from the same objective reality as others. Yet, through investigation we can get closer to the truth.

Ignorance is also not an excuse. Knowledge can be found through various sources, it might be knowledge by description, but it is still knowledge. Similarly, we are all ignorant of the future: every new event in our future is one we have no knowledge of. This is where the concept of intuition comes into consideration. In psychology, intuition encompasses the ability to know valid solutions to problem. For an example; Gary Klein found that under time pressure, high stakes, and changing parameters, experts use their base of experience to identify similar situations and intuitively choose feasible solutions. Thus, showing that the recognition primed decision model explains how people can make relatively fast decisions without having to compare options. Intuition is a pattern-matching process that quickly suggests possible courses of action. The analysis is the mental simulation, a conscious and deliberate review of the courses of action.

It should as be noted that Intuitive abilities were quantitatively tested at Yale University in the 1970s. While studying nonverbal communication, researchers noted that some subjects were able to read nonverbal facial cues before reinforcement occurred. In employing a similar design, they noted that highly intuitive subjects made decisions quickly but could not show their rationale. The knowledge of the past we carry with us grants us a tool against ignorance and gives us tools to intuit solutions to problems. We may not have absolute knowledge, but we are not disarmed by this. As we live in a shared reality we have a responsibility to, as Jedi we believe we have a responsibility to others and that includes ensuring we have knowledge: that we do not act on belief alone.

The Third Line: Passion and Serenity

Passion as an emotion is an intense one; often characterised by great enthusiasm or desire towards something or someone. Passion can take many forms, such as intellectual passions or the more obvious romantic or sexual passions. These can lead to positive outcomes or negative outcomes, depending on circumstance. In a positive light; passion can lead us to excel in our academic or technical field of choice, passions also play a part of having a healthy adult relationship. However, passion can lead us down dangerous paths just as easily. Some examples being that it can lead some to embrace and support an ideology based along irrational lines such as race; or it can lead to behaviour towards a person that is not wanted, stalking et cetera.

Strong emotion has a large part to play in our lives; it is what fuels our ability to fulfil our goals, as well as part of interpersonal relationships, and beside that is a part of our ability to make rational decisions. This importance is reflected in the work of Antonio Damasio; whom studied what occurred when the ties between the lower centres of the emotional brain and the thinking abilities of the neocortex are severed. Demasio found that despite emotions and feelings being able to cause discord or maladaptive thoughts reasoning; he found that the absence of emotion and feeling is no less damaging. Leading him to the position that feelings are typically indispensable for rational decisions. On this subject Demasion concluded that passions have a say on how the rest of the brain and cognition go about their business.

The impact of emotion, and thus passion, on our lives is evidently indispensable. Our emotions are part of our ability to think rationally, and our ability to fulfil our goals by giving us the necessary drive. A Jedi looks to improve himself through knowledge and training, in part passion plays a part in the early stages of this development. Without passion or want an individual would never find themselves travelling down the Jedi path, for there would be no impetus for this beginning.

As such, a Jedi looks to understand their own passion, their strong emotions, and we do this we explore why we experience such strong emotion: what is meaningful to us in the context we experience this emotion. A Jedi looks to understand the place of passion and desire in their thoughts, using it to explore what they find meaningful in life, the emotions serving as a contextual guide for this journey. A Jedi thus achieves serenity by never being in open conflict with their emotional self, rather by accepting it with an open heart and finding deeper meaning in what we are passionate about.

Emotional intelligence is one of the tools we use on the Jedi path; to find a synthesis of the two forces of reason and emotion, serenity, and passion- something that does away with the perceived tension between reason and feeling: finding the intelligent balance of the two.

The Fourth Line: Death and the Force

Death is both a beginning and an end, the end for the person whom has died and a beginning for those left behind. We shall not be discussing the metaphysical and the afterlife here. That is best left to the broader topic of the Force in totality.

Death, to those left behind, is a loss and each loss is fundamentally different. You will never talk to this person again, you can never again seek the comfort or challenges being with them presented. There is an ending there, they will never make choices again, they will never directly affect this world again by choice. They have faced their end.

Yet in a way they stay a part of the people they influenced. Having these people in your life will have shaped you somehow, made you the person you are. Ultimately here in lies the beginning mentioned earlier. If the memory of a person stays, they will always have an impact on our actions and our behaviours. They live on in the fact they shaped those around them, and in turn the lessons they gave others, shall pass on to those that come in generations to come.
We too are subject to this wheel and in time we shall die, and that will be our end, yet if we forge a strong connection with those around us, we can lead a meaningful life and we can leave a meaningful legacy.

Here we can now consider the Force: it is simply life, the connection between all people and all things, and the weight of the past and the potential for the future. As Jedi, we recognise ourselves to be part of the Force and that we carry forward the legacy of those before us. They are not gone in the sense we are products and proof of their existence and the impact of that existence. Our decedents will in turn be the same.

Thus, the Fifth Line is a reminder to us of our responsibility to life, and to preserve it. It is not a dismissal of the weight of death, or the certainty of the end. Rather it is to remind us that death is not an end, but part of a universal journey, one death does not end reality. Thus, death is not an end or beginning, it is a transition. There is a time someone does not exist or live, then they do, and then they do not again. They return to a state of nonexistence.

The concept of death is also often one that is often used to symbolise change: The Tarot, and various artistic works have explored death as a symbol of change. Death in the context of the Force can be interpreted as symbolic of transformation. On death one becomes one with the Force: a transformation. Through out life, we can experience many "deaths" of aspects of our identity: we become bored and disinterested in something that might have once dominated our daily lives. Sometimes we can get stuck in a pattern of mourning the past itself because we recognise a time, we were content, and that it has gone.

However, though things might pass, they have also been transformed. When something about us "dies" it is an important transformation that can be positive: the putting away of childish things, or something that was inherently unhealthy, can be key points in a person's life. Ultimately, life is a process of change and transformation, just as dying is a passing from life to death. As with the death of others, the death of things about ourselves, are something to live with and move on from.

The Mantra as a Whole

One should work to develop an over all understanding of the Mantra and how each line informs the other. Each line should be understood individual, and the language within, but each is inherently inapplicable to practical reality alone. One should also remember the Mantra applies to both the self and our external world.

Peace is both a means and an end to the Jedi: we want the world and our communities to be at peace, as much as we seek inner-peace and tranquillity for ourselves. Consider how understand our own emotional content may help us understand that of our external world. This needs self-knowledge, and reflection on our ignorance of our self. Consider how knowledge others have can help us, and how the ignorance of others can be dangerous. How can the strong passions of others cause disharmony: could we work to help people redirect their energies constructively? How in turn can such goals help us grow as people and find meaning. All the lines of the mantra inform all others: there is no situation where all the lines will not help inform you.

The Guidance Mantra

Originally devised by Jesse Bendyn (2008), for Tenebrae Surgunt, it was modified version of Costikyan Code (1987) better known as the Jedi Mantra. The code was originally as follows:

Control emotion to bring peace.
Gain knowledge to overcome ignorance.
Temper passion to gain serenity.
Death is not the end of life.

Below is an explanation of this mantra in the words of its original creator.

Control emotion to bring peace

Jedi are human. Every human feel emotion and Jedi are not exceptions. Jedi are in fact encouraged to feel their emotions, since compassion and kindness are central to our teachings. What we look to discourage is extreme emotions, both positive and negative. Extreme happiness can lead to detachment and arrogance as quickly as extreme pride can. What we look for here is a balance. Not too much positive and not too much negative. Negative emotions cannot be defeated, they will come back. It is the nature of the universe. What matters is what we do with those emotions. Do we let them have free reign inside us, or do we address ourselves to them? As Jedi we must face all our emotions and accept them, not just our positive but our negative as well. Only when they are balanced can we in fact become balanced. Balance brings peace to the soul.

Gain knowledge to overcome ignorance.

It is part of the human spirit to be curious. Even non-humans (such as animals, other kinds of beings) are found to have some degree of curiosity. It is curiosity that leads to new knowledge and new knowledge that leads to wisdom. Seeking knowledge helps a Jedi to understand all perspectives and points of view in a given situation. Perhaps the Jedi has been in the shoes of one or more parties. Knowledge is a tool by which we can better perceive and understand the universe around us.

Though seeking knowledge is not without its risks. A Jedi risks everything he or she already knows when they seek new truth. New truths sometimes falsify older knowledge that we only thought was true. A Jedi must never be afraid of stepping beyond and leaving behind a piece of knowledge. However, the Jedi must be very careful when doing this. He or she must be certain that this new knowledge is true. Anyways check before you step and look before you leap. Also, there is some knowledge that is dangerous to know. When facing something you think might be dangerous, seeking out guidance is highly recommended. A Jedi should never be afraid or ashamed to ask for help.

Temper passion to gain serenity

Passion is the will that drives us, the fire within our hearts. It is the steel of our tenacity and toughness. But as with emotion, the key is not extreme amounts, but balance. Use that fire to melt that steel into a keen sword, and you will find yourself powerful, yet able to rest. Extreme toughness can make you hard, solid, unmoving. It can cause fear as well. Many become too hard when they have been through great times of trial or pain and suffering. Usually the fire inside is diminished or even gone completely. Re-awakening this fire inside and restoring it to the same strength as the steel will ensure balance and serenity.

It is the same with extreme will. Extremely wilful individuals will have a hard time resting and listening to others. In this case meditation is the best answer. If you can wilfully calm your fires and gain some bit of wisdom to give your convictions a stable grounding, you will find yourself much more at peace, and much harder to push off your path. Sadly, sometimes for some individuals' bad consequences are required to bring the "steel" out of them. It is all an individual basis and it is all by choice. We can all choose to improve, or the universe can choose for us and teach us the hard way.

Death is not the end of life

New students may see the prospect of life after death to be a baseless belief in the sea of a factual universe. If you find yourself tending to agree with that, then part of following the Mantra is to accept such a belief as one of your own. However, in time and training you may begin to see this line a bit differently, as a statement of fact. Now, we all must make some sort of "leap of faith" to get anywhere in the universe. We make the "leap" that our feelings are true for the most part. As a Jedi you will learn to expand your perceptions and awaken a "sixth sense" in a manner of speaking. This is your ability to sense and use the Force. With time and training, you may begin to shift from belief, to assertion.

The Armonia Mantra

The Mantra as devised by Jesse Bendyn has since been revised into its current form by the Armonia Advisory Committee. It surmises our internal, meditative practices, and the tools of a Jedi. It is to serve as supplementary to the traditional Jedi Codes, and acts as a memorisation tools for the fundamental lessons within the Mantra:

Accept emotion to bring peace.
Seek knowledge to challenge ignorance.
Temper passions to find harmony.
Death is not the end of life.

Below is a brief explanation for each line, based contemporary understanding of the concepts:

Accept Emotion to bring Peace

A poor relationship with our emotional content is what often leads us to poor decisions. We look to accept our emotions for what they are, and to reflect upon their source, and why we are experiencing them. We accept our emotions as part of our cognitions, and as a part of us; they are not divisible from our reasoning process, or who we are.

Seek knowledge to challenge ignorance

We are not often aware we are ignorant until the moment we discover we are. It is thus our responsibility to pursue knowledge to challenge our own assumptions, and create routes for our own intellectual, and personal growth. Similarly; knowledge is power, and the best weapon we have against the ignorant actions of others. Understanding can be a source of peace, hard to find elsewhere.

Temper passions to find harmony

Discipline is the first freedom; often we have a poor relationship with our passions. We can fall into the trap of instant gratification, and thus chase activities, and other sources of immediate stimulation. We can ultimately fail at what we hate, as much as what we love. As such; we temper our passions, actions we find most meaningful, and what gives us energy into a reliable way to orientate our lives. Through doing so, we can pursue meaning, and find harmony.

Death is not the end of life

To some a metaphysical statement, however, it is quite literal. A death is but one death, and a part of life; we spend a long time not existing before we did, and we are simply returning to a state of non-existence. When we die, we shall leave memories, and we have but one chance at life: it is not a rehearsal. We must strive to live a meaningful life, for both ourselves, and those we leave behind. Similarly, we must also remember that death comes for us all, and that the deaths we experience in our lives do not stop the world turning. We must be ready to carry on.

For use in Meditation

The Mantra can also be used in meditation using the below format. Breath in on the first statement of each line, and out on the second:

Accept Emotion > Peacefulness
Seek Knowledge > Understanding
Temper Passion > Harmony
Mourn Death > Embrace Life
You may find it useful to mouth or even speak the second statement when you exhale.

ASSIGNMENTS:

1. Looking over the Jedi Mantras provided in this module, which line do you feel is the most difficult to live by? Why do you feel this way, and how do you think you can work on incorporating it into your life?

2. Compare the mantra to another: note similarities, and differences. Discuss critically the mantra and its contents: how useful is it as a meditation tool?

Instructions for Final Paper

Your final paper must be a minimum of 5 pages (not including Title and Source pages), double-spaced, Times New Roman 12pt Font and include a minimum of 5 sources (10 is preferred) in APA Format.

TOPIC: Research a deity of your choice. Could be Abrahamic, Greek, Japanese, Igbo, Aztec, Maori, etc. In your paper, please answer the following questions-

1) What kinds of decisions does this deity make?

2) How, in the stories surrounding him/her, has their decisions impacted man?

3) Using the Armonia Jedi Code* (if you are a member of another Jedi Order, you may use the code of the order you hail from), discuss whether or not you feel this deity's character might ask you to do something that violates the Jedi Code.

4) Finally, discuss how you would deal with a situation if this deity came to you and asked you to do something which went directly against the Jedi Code.

*If you have chosen to receive a certification with your studies, you may choose to use a Jedi Code that is not Armonia's- to include the Heartland Jedi Code spoken of this in Module, or the code of your own Jedi Order. Armonia immediately recognizes the variant codes used at the following Jedi Orders:

Force Academy

Temple of the Jedi Order

Temple of the Jedi Force

You may choose to the use the fictional codes themselves, or develop your own. If you choose to use one that is not already accepted, you may write us at armoniaseminary@gmail.com for us to review it against the fictional codes, discuss with you any improvements and approve your code at no cost.

Meditation on the Mantra

For the next two weeks, take some time to meditate with the Armonia Mantra, as outlined below. This module will provide you with space for the the first week of your meditation to write down notes of how the Mantra has impacted you, and you will have space in the next module for week 2. In Module 2, you will also be asked to explain what your overall experience with using this mantra has been.

Breath in on the first statement of each line, and out on the second:

Accept Emotion > Peacefulness
Seek Knowledge > Understanding
Temper Passion > Harmony
Mourn Death > Embrace Life

You may find it useful to mouth or even speak the second statement when you exhale. Do this for a minimum of 5 minutes each time. If you have completed the "The Spiritual Art of Meditation" by Alethea Thompson, we recommend that you do this mantra in accordance with the time of day that proved the most effective for you when you completed the module on Chants & Mantras.

Mantra Mediation Journal, Day 1 Notes

Mantra Mediation Journal, Day 2 Notes

Mantra Mediation Journal, Day 3 Notes

Mantra Mediation Journal, Day 4 Notes

Mantra Mediation Journal, Day 5 Notes

Mantra Mediation Journal, Day 6 Notes

Mantra Mediation Journal, Day 7 Notes

Notes

The Jedi Code: A Jedi's True Ally?

Module Two

Understanding the Jedi Creed

The Creed (Cerasini, 1999), or Skywalker Code, holds an unusual place in the world of Jedi Realism. Published in the middle of the genesis of early Jediism, it has not readily displaced the Jedi Mantra, yet it has been a part of Jedi Realism since it started. To be objective we must recognise that The Jedi Praxeum came into existence in 95, The Jedi of the New Millennium in 97, Jedi Academy in 98, and Jedi Creed by 99. Thus, the forerunners of the Jedi Realist movement had begun their first works by 1999.

However, the zenith of the early movement was arguably 2001, when the BBC (British Broadcasting Company) ran the Story "The Gospel According to Luke Skywalker" in that year: arguably the first major news story run on the Jedi Community. Similarly, it was not until 2002 that internet penetration (the availability of the internet) reached over 50% in the United States where the largest, by percent, of Jedi still live. As such, the Jedi community as a broader collective has always lived with the Skywalker Code, and the Creed has informed the notion of being a Jedi as much as the Mantra.

To understand the Creed, we shall focus on the key statements and phrases about being a Jedi that scale to reality and are consistent across both versions of the Creed that exist. Statements about the galaxy and ruling over others through supernatural power evidently do not scale to reality, and thus can be distracting rather than informative.

Guardians of Peace

"Jedi do not fight for peace. That is only a slogan and is as misleading as slogans always are. Jedi fight for civilization, because only civilization creates peace. We fight for justice because justice is the fundamental bedrock of civilization: an unjust civilization is built upon sand. It does not long survive a storm." —Mace Windu, Shatterpoint (Stover, 2004)

Above is a quote by Mace Windu from the novel Shatterpoint, and in some respects it is in fact representative of how many Jedi Realists view the notion of being a Guardian of Peace. One cannot guard peace directly, for peace is something achieved through the various mechanisms of civilisation and just society. To protect peace, one must identify and guard these mechanisms. This is how a Jedi guards' peace in reality: we work towards ensuring our community is a stable community, and one where justice prevails. We work towards equity, and to ensure as great a degree of fairness as we can. Life is not fair, but all that means to a Jedi is that we ourselves must work to be fair. Furthermore, a Jedi must realize that peace is fragile and as impermanent as everything else. To keep peace, one does not prepare for war: one prepares for peace. That means one must be prepared to work for it, and in times of conflict be prepared to work to restore peace.

We treasure peace because it allows freedom, it allows competition, it allows debate, and it allows diversity. Peace is a space within which growth can occur, and where people can exist as they choose. War, conflict, and the use of violence undoes all that. Conflict leads to tribalism, and ideology based on clinging to the familiar and to the similar at the expense of all others. Conflict needs a conceited mind concerned with what is other from the self. That is why Jedi strive for peace: it is a means and an end.

Be wary though that although peace is created by civilisation, one must not develop an attachment towards the institutions or towards an idealised version of the society one serves. Peace preserved at the expense of others creates an unjust society. Peace preserved, by means of compromising certain values, is not a sustainable peace. A Jedi is loyal to what preserves peace, not the mechanisms that help to do so in society.

Powers to defend and protect

A misunderstood sentiment at best, and one often explored one-dimensionally through the notion of self-defence and violence. To defend and to protect is often interpreted in reactive means in such scenarios, and the line becomes blurred when the notion of pre-emptive strikes is brought up: is not striking when you have enough certainty that you or others are in physical danger permissible? Ultimately, yes: if you have sufficient belief that you are in imminent danger, then you prevent it is to defend and protect yourself and others.

However, the lesson is much broader than simple violence: what of poverty, hunger, and various other ills. A Jedi works to defend and protect others against these as well, and in all these things we know that prevention is superior to a cure in achieving long lasting and sustainable results. Defend and protect does not imply passivity or awaiting the apparent threat: as Jedi we use our skills to help our community directly, and if we can strengthen our community, it is more resilient to problems. Though we might rally to the aid of some one in peril, ultimately, what we do day to day is how we best defend and protect.

Note, the word powers: now, as human beings we do not possess the supernatural abilities of the Jedi of the fiction. However, we all have power, and powers as a word needs consideration as it is a moralising statement. Power is the ability to do something or act in a certain way, and this extends to the ability to influence others or a course of events. As Jedi, we use our power by defending and protecting others: we have a responsibility to how we use our power. Our power can serve us, but we also look for our power to aid others.

Respect all life

Life has many forms and there are many forms of respect. The Force is the connection between all things: Respect for life is the recognition of the connection between the self and everything around you and accepting that our actions always have consequences.

With the above said Jedi are not naive, and understand that adversity, disagreement, iniquity, conflict, and suffering do happen. However, we believe that the destruction of the well-being and happiness of others cannot bring one's own, for it brings unfortunate consequences that would be unnecessary if one simply practiced respect for others.

Yet, sometimes criminals do prosper, and sometimes cruelty seems to earn reward, but ultimately that creates enemies and ultimately one becomes concerned with the past rather than enjoying the present. A person is the company they keep, and if they keep many body guards that says something about them, as does refusing to keep the company of any one.

For a Jedi, respect is continuing to acknowledge that connection between ourselves and others and giving it due deference. Respect is shown by trying to avoid needless actions, and by remembering that others have the same right to existence as we do, and the same treatment and dignity we would wish for ourselves and our loved ones.

Serve others rather than ruling

The answer is simple: A Jedi knows that all life is important and should be cherished. To rule over it would reduce the freedoms that all life has. The only way to help is to lead a good path, and to protect what is good. We also recognise that no matter what we do we still are connected to others, and ultimately, we serve a role no matter what we do. Even in positions of authority we inherently serve a system: we cannot avoid being in service to something. Thus, we look to make our service meaningful by embracing what we serve regardless: other people.

We are also called to not impose our ideals on others: our ideals are our own, and we can expect them to be followed only by fellow Jedi. For Jedi, it is important to remember that even if others do things which you consider immoral or unethical, you must consider it in context: is that a cultural normality, and is it something you truly think is wrong or is it simply something you would not do yourself? If it is harming another against their will, that is a different matter, but ultimately the actions of others are their own, and should be respected as such.

Improve themselves through knowledge and training

Jedi improve themselves so that they may help others. The knowledge you gain and the training you undergo allow you to help others. Without training, and proper knowledge you would be unprepared and unable to help others. This part of the code reminds us that we must always aspire to be competent when we confront problems or offer to help others. It also reminds us of the need to consistently learn, and to aspire to improve ourselves.

If we lack knowledge, and training, and confront issues without preparation and forethought we can simply create further issues. Rushing to an emergency without proper training and equipment can lead to simply becoming a further casualty. Offering to help someone with a matter you have no knowledge of could further confuse the matter. The intent to be helpful does not automatically mean you may be helpful: having the right knowledge and training is what makes one helpful.

ASSIGNMENTS:

Looking over the different lines of the Jedi Creed, explain which one you feel best expresses the way you wish to manifest your Jedi Path. How do the lines around it inform the line you have chosen? Your answer must be 250 words minimum (not including citations, if any)

Mantra Mediation Journal, Day 1 Notes

Mantra Mediation Journal, Day 2 Notes

Mantra Mediation Journal, Day 3 Notes

Mantra Mediation Journal, Day 4 Notes

Mantra Mediation Journal, Day 5 Notes

Mantra Mediation Journal, Day 6 Notes

Mantra Mediation Journal, Day 7 Notes

ASSIGNMENT

Explain how meditating on the Armonia Mantra has affected your last two weeks. Your answer should be 150 words minimum (not including citations, if any).

Notes

Notes

The Jedi Code: A Jedi's True Ally?

Module Three

The Jedi Behaviours

In 1996 the Tales of the Jedi Companion for the Star Wars: The Roleplaying Game was published. The book is interesting as it has a section on how to role-play a Jedi called the Jedi way, and how a game master should referee Jedi Characters. Though, not a significant contributor to later Jedi realism and Jediism it was an influence on the early Jedi community when the line between role-play and actual adherence to the Jedi Path was blurred.

In 2002 the Power of the Jedi Sourcebook was released for the Star Wars Roleplaying Game published by Wizards of the Coast. Within the book several behaviours outlined how a Player should effectively roleplay a Jedi. These behaviours became relatively well known among the Jedi, due to continued entanglement with Roleplaying, and even now they are easily found on the Wookiepedia page for the Jedi Code by many aspiring Jedi and those simply curious.

Interestingly, the behaviours are very similar to the works of several Jedi Realists: The 21 Maxims (Chanada, 2001), The 16 Basic Teachings of the Jedi (Kidohdin, 2003), The Jedi Circle (Trout, 2005), and the Community project The Jedi Compass (The Jedi Community, 2015) which can be found in this work book. Some cite the behaviours as obvious inspiration for said works, however simultaneous development, and the fact the format is effective for expanding on the otherwise anaemic sources of the Mantra and the Creed without contradicting said sources are also suitable explanations. Either way, knowledge of the behaviours can help further understand the logic of the Mantra and Creed, even if they are designed for Role-Play.

Of course, The Jedi Way from Tales of the Jedi, and the behaviours from the Power of the Jedi Sourcebook cannot be presented here, as copyright material. However, below are three documents called Being a Living Jedi, Jedi Wisdom and The Jedi Perspective which were based on the Jedi Behaviours, and originally written for the Tenebrae Surgunt Jedi Group

Being a Living Jedi

When one avows him, or her, self to the Jedi Code, they at once accept a set of responsibilities and obligations they are supposed to fulfil.

Community Service
The Jedi exist to serve the greater good, and part of this is through rendering community service. A Jedi must always make him, or her, self-available for volunteer work, and in theory should look to have a regular outlet to allow them to use their skills to aid the community.

Supply Aid
A Jedi is obliged to help those in need of aid whenever possible and are expected to have the ability to prioritise. This does not mean a Jedi is to abandon other goals in every circumstance should a situation arrive, however a Jedi must do his or her best to make sure that they are of aid to those who were most in need of aid.

Protect the Weak
A Jedi is expected to defend those who cannot defend themselves. However, a Jedi should always remain mindful of cultural and individual differences, even if they are against the Jedi moral and ethical codes. Though a Jedi is expected to protect the weak, he, or she, is also expected to choose his/her battles, and to be mindful of all possibilities.

Give support
The greatest impact a Jedi can make is in empowering others to rise above the challenges they face. Even though a Jedi may believe he/she could do a superior job, sometimes it is best to let others rise to challenges, and to let communities heal themselves.

The Jedi Perspective

"The Jedi Perspective is how a Jedi views the world and his or her place in it. A Jedi's life is service to those in need, and he or she realises that the needs of the world take priority over his or her personal needs. A Jedi therefore places life and justice above his or herself. A Jedi is humble and does not seek fame or power. He or she instead appreciates the beauty of the world and the universe and seeks to preserve that beauty." – Jesse Bendyn.

To reach the lofty ideal espoused, we must ask how a Jedi develops their perspective. The most basic and fundamental element of the Jedi perspective is therefore that of Self-Discipline.

Overcome Arrogance
Jedi must learn that, although we aspire to great ideals, we are not fundamentally better than those who do not. You must remember you are only a Jedi because someone has taken the trouble to teach you, and you have been given the opportunity by virtue of locality, and financial status.

Moderate Confidence
No matter one's abilities, never begin to believe in your own infallibility or the security of your position. Many have failed by virtue of overestimating their own capabilities. Remember to always be mindful of your flaws with regards to your work, and abilities, and to remember there is no shame in needing the aid of others.

Overcome Pessimism
Defeatism is just as dangerous as overconfidence. You must always aim for success; but allow for the possibility of failure. Never allow yourself a fatalistic attitude; if something occurs there was a reason. Never be content with adequacy, and the cold comfort of being able to say you tried.

Overcome Stubbornness
It is always best to end things peacefully than to win or lose. One should simply look to never lose, that means to never lose to yourself. Stubbornness beyond reason serves no one, so one must always keep their mind open to compromise.

Overcome Recklessness
Speed does not necessarily lead to success, as being the first somewhere does not always equal success. Though it is to better act and err, than it is to let the moment of action pass; it is better to wait on said moment, then to create one needlessly. A Jedi should practice patience and having a broad perspective, rather than suffering narrow vision due to a lack of self-discipline.

Control Curiosity
Although, there may come times one must delve into discreet matters, and the secrets of others, it should never become a matter of course. A Jedi should never use an opportunity to delve for the sake of curiosity. A Jedi should always restrain himself outside ethical needs.

Overcome Aggression
Aggression and violence serve to alienate, and to disrupt communities. However, if a Jedi trains to be a defender of others, how can he stop violence without aggression? A Jedi must learn to act with intent, through training, and discipline. Not through reliance on base instincts.

Moderate Materialism
Though we are not subject to the structures of the fictional Jedi, we are neither awarded their boons and benefits. A real Jedi requires possessions to live in this world; however, they would still be wise to avoid attachment to objects, and to become embroiled in the pursuit of artifice. A Jedi should restrain him, or her, self to what is needed.

Jedi Wisdom

A wise Jedi is mindful of his, or her, responsibilities and attends to them.

Be Honest
Dishonesty is a course of action that is disrespectful and lacks integrity. If at all possible, a Jedi must avoid deception. Although, a Jedi may find themselves requiring deception as a tool, it should only be resorted to with ethical reasoning, and as a last resort.

Keep your Promises
If you make a promise, always be prepared to keep it, or else make amends. Thus, you should never make a promise you are not certain you can keep. It is important to remember this, as it speaks of your reliability, and integrity. Should people lose faith in either, it can be impossible to regain.

Uphold the Law
Jedi must be mindful of the law, and like any citizens are expected to follow the law, as we expect others to. Even though our philosophies may not agree with some laws we encounter, there are few ethical justifications for breaking the law. Even under such cases, a Jedi should not consider themselves an exception to a rule, simply because of a title, or a code.

Respect Life
Jedi believe killing under any circumstance is essentially wrong. Though we may be able to create ad hoc self-justification in hindsight, we must remember that no matter the reason, murder and killing is wrong. However, we must also remember to forgive, and to remember we do not live in a perfect world. The possibility of a completely clean life from this matter is nigh on impossible. A Jedi honours life, by preserving it where they can, and not conflating murder with values such as justice.

Honour your fellow Jedi
Your fellow Jedi are your colleagues and compatriots; your actions reflect on them, as theirs reflect upon you. Should you perform badly, it would take much

effort off them to reform the image you would produce, and vice versa. Furthermore, we are a team, and a hierarchy. You must respect your teachers, and leaders, and they must respect you, as you should respect your student. Therefore, it is important to always keep in mind how you reflect your fellow Jedi, and to act as an example for how you hope they will reflect the Jedi.

ASSIGNMENT

Choose one of the sections outlined in this module (Being a Living Jedi, The Jedi Prospective, or Jedi Wisdom) and explain how the Jedi Creed outlined in Module 2 relates to it. Your answer must be 250 words minimum (not including citations, if any)

What Does the Jedi Code Say?

Over the next few weeks you will be given one topic and one scenario to analyze what you believe guidance you can take from the Jedi Code. This is meant to be a contemplative exercise, and as such your mind can go a myriad of directions. To really understand a Jedi Code, however, you'll need to stick to one code throughout the duration of this course.

With each topic/scenario, identify the line(s) of the Jedi Code which inform your opinion. Don't rush the answers either. Take some time during the week to meditate on what is being said before you make a decision.

It is of note, that the Jedi believe in personal adoption of a code. We do not believe in forcing others to adopt the Jedi Way of life, of course that doesn't mean that we don't draw a line in the sand and say "no more" (but that's for another workbook). So when you're contemplating the Jedi Code, do it from the prospective of what it is telling you to do- and not what it's telling non-Jedi to do. That is, when we ask about Abortion, the question is whether or not it's something you personally, as a Jedi following this code, can you (assuming you have a functional womb) undergo an abortion procedure. Or if you are unable to bear children, as a Jedi following this code, could you support your partner having an abortion.

Again, we aren't asking what you want to believe, we're asking you to use the Jedi Code to justify your answer. At the end of the day, you and the Jedi Code itself may be at odds with one another- but if we are to be Jedi, we need to know what it is we are signing on for.

You'll need to write down your thoughts and turn them in to your teacher/mentor.

SHOULD A JEDi...
Be Vegetarianism/Veganism based solely on the belief of Animal Rights and the jedi code?

SCENARIO

Your parents (regardless of your own age) have separated, and they are trying to turn you against the other parent.

Notes

The Jedi Code: A Jedi's True Ally?

Module Four

Loyalty to the Code

"A Jedi is bound by the code. By maintaining your loyalty to the code, you are able to keep your actions in check through the moral integrity of the Jedi Path outlined in the Jedi Code. It is important that a Jedi checks their own version of the code against the original codes (Jedi Code and Skywalker Code) before they adopt it." – The Jedi Compass (2015)

The foundation of the Jedi Realist community, and Jediism, the Jedi Mantra and Creed have supplied a guide for living to Jedi for over two decades and have been a source of transformative experiences. Many examples of this can be found in the text; the Jedi Compass, as well as by many documents scattered about the community. Yet, there are several structural and conceptual issues with both the Mantra and the Creed.

Issues of the Jedi Mantra:

1. It is a collection of propositional statements which do not identify what is necessary, and what is sufficient, for the statements to be true.
2. The statements are presented as a collection of related concepts, however, the relationship between each line is not explicitly addressed.

Issues of the Jedi Creed:

1. Statements which do not scale to reality; they are grounded in the role of the fictional Jedi, and their abilities.
2. Absolute statements reliant on undefined terms, which lack the flexibility to apply to reality.

The issues with the Jedi Mantra and Creed extend beyond those identified above, with most argument sand critiques being content based rather than structural. Jedi realists have long recognised issues with the Mantra and Creed and taken different approaches to revolving them.
Two distinct approaches are most notable:

A. Robust training regime: The creed and/or mantra are placed within context, and the issues and critiques directly addressed through the training regime, and with additional documents.

An example of this approach would be the Jedi Behaviors discussed in Module 3. These were set up to assist Jedi in understanding how to best use the Jedi Code. This approach has been taken by several real world Jedi Orders, such as Temple of the Jedi Order: whom have adopted the 21 Maxims (Chanada, 2001), The 16 Basic Teachings of the Jedi (Kidohdin, 2003), and developed their own creed based on the Prayer of Saint Francis to expand on the meaning of the Jedi mantra, and to outline their dogma.

B. Replace the Creed and/or Mantra with an original composition: A new document is created which reflects the same values but lacks the structural or content-based issues discussed.

An example of this can be found in the fiction. There are two different versions of the Fictional Jedi Mantra. The story goes, that the original Jedi Mantra went "A, yet B", but upon seeking to clarify this code, Udan-Urr changed it to "There is no A, there is B". Even in terms of the Jedi Creed, there is an alteration made by Luke Skywalker which begins with understanding the importance of a Jedi's promise.

A real world example would be the approach of the Heartland Jedi; whom developed their own original creed in its entirety, without an explicit reference to the Jedi Mantra or Creed, but rather grounding their creed in the experience and expectations of their members. Below is this code:

1. I am a Jedi, a guardian of peace.
2. I acknowledge all life is sacred.
3. I choose to serve others,
4. I use my training to defend and protect, never to assault.
5. I will present a professional demeanour.
6. I will be mindful of my thoughts and control my actions.
7. I know myself and am aware of my surroundings.
8. I will approach all situations holistically.

9. I will seek knowledge with the understanding of self-ignorance.
10. I will find peace in the midst of a storm.
11. It is through understanding of the Force I am transformed.

As can be seen; the structure is quite different, but has a similar message, and has the core values expressed in the original Jedi codes. Armonia Seminary has taken the middle road: we acknowledge and use the original Mantra and the Skywalker Code (The Creed). However, we make use of our own creed and mantra which are intended to explicitly expand on the original codes, and we consider them equally valid to the original codes when discussing Jedi behaviour and belief.

Our code serves several purposes; to guide our members in their understanding of the Jedi path and teachings, but to also serve as a mission statement, and a statement of Armonia's core values. It is the journey of the practitioner, and the intent of our pedagogy.

The Creed:

1. We are Jedi; Protectors of Freedom
2. We respect our connected world
3. Thus, we serve others
4. By leading through example
5. By acting with integrity
6. We stay strong to support others
7. We strive for growth with our actions
8. We face adversity with wisdom and knowledge
9. We are one with the Force

Source of the Creed:

The Creed is derived from statements made by a collection of individuals, whose joint experiences within the Jedi community amount to at least half a century. The first step to develop the code; was to ask those involved to outline the core values they feel are essential to their life as a Jedi. The statements collected were:

1. Accept challenge as learning, help all able, never stop.
2. One with the Force, go beyond, improve, and irradiate.
3. I choose to serve, protect, and defend others.
4. Honour, Educate, Love and Protect.
5. We seek strength to support others.
6. Respect, Competence, Responsibility, and Integrity.

The Creed as individual statements:

The most direct means to understand the creed, is to first understand each line, and the terms within them as we intend them to be understood. Below is a brief explanation of each of the lines, and the terms used within them. Keep in mind that no single line should be considered separate from the context of the rest of the creed, however, each line is crucial in its own way.

1. Jedi are protectors of freedom: Peace facilitates debate and growth for all, and the opportunity to be an individual. The cornerstone of peace is freedom, and fairness.

Jedi thus, at first principle, protect the freedoms of those they protect and seek fairness in their dealings and in their interventions.

2. Jedi perceive, and respect, the connected world: Human interactions and experiences are a series of actions and reactions. Jedi recognise the relationships between individuals, their communities, and the environments we share. Jedi respect this profound connection, and it forms the basis of the Jedi path; we are all but parts of an organic machine, each with our contribution to make, but also with a capacity to cause harm. Thus, Jedi maintain a mindset of being mindful of how our actions connect us to others; in ways, we cannot always fathom.

3. Jedi serve others: Jedi do not practice Comtean Altruism; a philosophy grounded in the ends justifying the means, so long as the means is the good of others. Jedi do not presume to know the "good" of others and try to preserve

the freedom to strive for a person's own good so long as it harms no other. Therefore, Jedi serve; with respect to the connection between all, to facilitate the individual's ability to strive for good in their own lives. Only through service can this be achieved; not through self-righteous intervention, or command.

4. Jedi lead through example: This can also be read as Jedi teach through example; though the first call is to serve, it also falls on a Jedi to teach others, and to lead their fellow Jedi. Also; a Jedi can help others by being an example of a well-adjusted life. A Jedi must keep in mind that what she or he does affects others, and they will judge; as such a Jedi must act to the best of their ability always, and be the example needed.

5. Jedi act with integrity: A Jedi must act with competency, they should not endanger others by taking on tasks they are unfit for. They must act with honesty; dishonesty for dishonesty's sake or for gain often with time brings only mistrust and an unassailable challenge, and great harm to all involved. Jedi must act with respect and act with consent in helping others; a Jedi must involve those they help in their own struggle, but also make them aware of why an action is being taken. Only through this can a person learn and be free.

6. Jedi stay strong to support others: This is achieved through training, study, and engaging in meaningful activities. A Jedi must be competent if they are to be of assistance in an emergency, or even just in general times of difficulty. However, a Jedi must also maintain their own sense of self and maintain the energy they need. If they do not they in danger of being unable to live a functional life, and without that foundation they will be unable to support others.

7. Jedi strive for growth through their actions: Each experience is an opportunity to learn, and to progress; for all involved. In resolving a situation Jedi seeks to set a foundation for growth; by illuminating for those involved the lessons to be learned, and by creating a harmonious solution allowing all to reflect effectively, and move forward from the situation as it stood. Through this; a Jedi can hopefully prevent a repeating situation, but also ensure those connected do not go on to cause further disruption and problems.

8. Jedi face adversity with wisdom and knowledge: When confronted with a problem a Jedi first appeals to sensibility; they seek to appreciate the complex factors of a situation. They maintain an eye for dangers, and weigh them accordingly. They also appeal to sources of knowledge and experience to determine the right course of action.

9. Jedi are one with the Force: Jedi are the bridge between the visible and the invisible. The Force is a by-word for the connection of all life; the nature of actions and their consequences on others. The ineffable reality that exists between individuals and their surroundings. A Jedi knows they are part of this connection, and strive to be aware of this connection. The word Force reminds us that our actions have an energy, and that energy will find a pathway to expression; we are not free from the consequences of our actions. We and our actions are one in the same, and as such we are one with the Force. However, it is easy to neglect this thinking, and become unaware of the "Force", and this line also reminds us that awareness is our most essential tool.

The Creed as a Narrative:

The Armonia Creed should also be understood as a narrative, with an internal set of consequential logic.

1. We are Jedi; Protectors of Freedom
2. We respect our connected world

The above identifies the role of a Jedi, and the central tenet of being a Jedi; above is what our intended goal is, to protect freedom, and why we do so; we respect the connections of our world.

3. Thus, we serve others
4. By leading through example
5. By acting with integrity

The above identifies how we intend to achieve our goal and explains the consequences of our respecting the connections of this world. We serve others because of our respect for the world, and we defend freedom through action reflecting our goals, and with integrity when pursuing said goal.

6. We stay strong to support others
7. We strive for growth with our actions
8. We face adversity with wisdom and knowledge
9. We are one with the Force

The above are the result of our actions as outlined in the prior segment. If we act with integrity, and lead through example, this is what we can achieve in our own lives, and the lives of others. However, it is not a single directional relationship. These values are also what empower us to lead through example, and act with integrity. How we achieve our intended ends, is not distinct from the means we employ. Our goals are what orientate our actions, but the value of our goals is set by what we will do to achieve them.

Assessment:
You can answer using your own code of choice, and/or the Armonia code. (Recommended Length 150 words for each assignment).
1. Identify the source, and original context of the code. Identify values reflected in the code that are found in the original context.
2. Explore a line from the Code, and identify the qualifying elements, and define key words. What is necessary or sufficient for the statement to be true? Is it found in another line?
3. What is the narrative of the code? Identify, and discuss critically the consequential logic, if it has any, of the code.
4. Apply the code: are there any elements of the code you feel already impacts on your life? Identify and explain your reasoning.

SHOULD A JEDI...

Be an active Participant in Abortion?

SCENARIO

Your best friend ("L") calls you crying that their 20 year old child ("N") has started doing meth. "L" knows that "N" typically hangs out with another methhead named "M". So "L" asks you to go to "M"'s house and pull "N" back to his/her senses.

Notes

Notes

The Jedi Code: A Jedi's True Ally?

Module Five

Ethical Guidelines, and Procedures

In most services and industries, there are individuals concerned with the ethical implications, and potential legal ramifications, of the actions of employees. In the world of research; there are ethics boards who exist purely to ensure that research is, as their title implies, ethical. In the world of health care; professionals are held to ethics standards intended to protect the dignity of those in care. In the academic world; there are boards on academic honesty, and which concern themselves with the upright behaviour of students and scholars. In any service, where the well-being of a living being is in the hands of an employee of said service, there will be an ethics process. In any industry where the misuse, or misrepresentation, of information, can be damaging; there usually exists some form of oversight. Even in countries which have free-press; this does not give the press freedom to defame, and journalists have found themselves brought to account for misrepresenting the truth about individuals. Around the world, even in countries which respect the human right to free speech, the damage that can be caused by hate speech is increasingly accepted; and individuals have faced criminal charges for the use of language to incite violence and discrimination.

Some industries have historical ethics codes and guides, and a well-known and oft cited code is that of the Hippocratic Oath; a code attributed to Hippocrates and historically taken by western physicians for centuries, with some medical schools continuing to advocate a modified form of the oath to this day. However, such an example is a historical exception to a rule, and it is only in the modern day that most industries employ an ethics guide, rather than rely solely on the law and good judgement of its employees. The question that arises from this thus becomes; why do ethical issues arise at all? Why have human beings through the ages found a need to codify their ethics, and in the modern era have ethics codes become a standard practice for services and industries. There are several, short, arguments for why ethical issues arise:

1. Human beings, and non-human animals experience feelings: they are living, sentient, creatures. These feelings include pain and fear.

2. Human beings are thinking creatures: though a situation may not cause physical harm or injury, it may cause distress from feelings or thoughts aroused by the situation.

3. Purposefully causing another harm is usually held to be morally unacceptable by society: To induce the above thoughts, and feelings mentioned above, or to cause physical injury, to an individual is disruptive and generally destructive.

In the everyday experience; regardless of the situation, the individual encounters their fellow human beings, and non-sentient animals, on a regular basis. Ethical dilemmas arise because of the unavoidable interactions between individuals; especially in services, or situations, where the individual is the focus. An example where people are the focus being the care industry; an example in which people are often left very vulnerable. As such, there are several abstract benefits to an ethical code, that benefit both employees and employers, and protect all parties involved from harm:

1. Protection from legal ramifications: a robust ethics code should prevent harm from occurring, and thus responsibility for any harm that occurs. It should protect the recipient of a service from receiving unethical, better read as harmful, treatment.

2. If an employee follows the guide, they should be protected by the guide: if they act within its restrictions, and according to their training, then any liability does not fall on them but on the lack of foresight of their employer.

3. Conversely to point 2: if a company has a clear ethics guide, and an employee acts against it and causes harm then the responsibility falls on the recklessness of that employee.

4. Builds trust between the public and the company: a transparent ethics code reassures individuals that their rights are respected, and they have a means of recourse if any harm befalls them due to the negligence of the company.

A service is only so strong as its customer base, and a service only so secure as its most careless worker. An ethics guide supplies a safety net for both sides of the relationship in any industry; the employee and the customer.

An example of an ethics code with far reaching implications is that of the British Psychological Society (BPS); members of the BPS, be they practicing psychologists, or scholars of psychology, are expected to adhere to it. As such, it has ramifications in the spheres of care and academia. The Code of Ethics and Conduct (BPS, 2006) is constructed around four major ethic principles. I have outlined these principles and the implications, in brief, on the psychologist below:

A. Respect: This is respect for the individual and their rights, such as their privacy, and self-determination, and acknowledging that we only treat or test with consent, and that the individual can withdraw this consent at any time.

B. Competence: Knowing how to work ethically, and to understand the limits of one's own competence. That to work outside the realm of one's training and competence is dangerous, and probably harmful.

C. Responsibility: Actively protecting patients and research participants from harm and working to prevent the misuse or abuse of the contributions of themselves to society.

D. Integrity: Honesty, avoiding exploitation, defusing conflicts of interest, and keeping proper personal boundaries. In general, addressing, and challenging ethical issues, and any misconduct.

The BPS Code shows how broad, and far reaching, such ethics guidelines can be. These principles do not halt at the door to the office, but permeate the entirety of a psychologist's professional life, and this can be true of guidelines in general. Increasingly, the workplace is moralised, and the dangers of not regulating or at least guiding behaviour has been made clear by the failings of the past. One can also hopefully recognise parallels between the Armonia Creed and the Ethics code discussed:

"Jedi perceive, and respect, the connected world."

We respect the harm our actions can cause to others, if we act improperly, or poorly; especially if someone has come to us for aid.

"Jedi act with integrity."
We stay mindful of our competencies; we strive to be honest to others, and ourselves, about our capabilities. We reflect on our successes and failures and look to take the correct action when called to.

"Jedi stay strong to support others."
We act responsibly by ensuring we are fit for the tasks at hand; if we are unwell, or unfit for the tack, we do not take it upon ourselves. We can do more harm than good by trying to help when we are unfit to do so.

Hopefully, this has, in brief illustrated the benefits of having an ethics code, and how the Armonia Creed can aid you in professional life. That it does not contradict the real world but has very real advice to give on living effectively.

ASSIGNMENTS:

1A. Does your current profession have an ethics code? Please outline in brief (150 words recommended). If your current industry lacks an explicit ethics code, proceed to 1B.

1B. Find and outline, in brief and in your own words, an ethics code for an industry or volunteer role you would be interested in pursuing (150 words recommended).

2. How do you feel the Jedi Code (The Armonia Code or your favoured Code) benefits, or perhaps impedes, you in the work place? (150 words recommended).

3. We have outlined benefits of an ethics code here; can you think of any difficulties such codes could cause? (3 Bullet-Points recommended.)

SHOULD A JEDI…

Carry a legal, deadly, weapon for Self-Defense (gun, knife, per your country's laws)?

SCENARIO

A friend of yours has recently entered into a relationship with someone. Since the relationship started, you noticed this individual shows signs of abuse; however, when approached they are unwilling to admit anything is going on.

Notes

The Jedi Code: A Jedi's True Ally?

Module Six

Statements of Values

In the chapters prior we discussed the notion of ethical guidelines, with the BPS code of ethics used as an example. However, we discussed the core values of said ethics guide, rather than the guide in its totality. Yet, guidelines are built around core values; after all, if you do not understand the ethical principles, how can you apply them in a practical, directed manner. As such, we shall now look at that starting point; statements of values, or value statements. In recent years, statements of values have become a focal point of the industrial and volunteer world, as well as the healthcare world. Many organisations and groups now publish their values; a value statement explains what the organisation, or its leaders to be more specific, believe in, and from a practical perspective is really a set of values that articulates what they expect of their members.

Like ethical guidelines; these value statements inform the individuals beholden to it of what their expected behaviours are. A useful analogy is taking a train with other passengers; the company, or team, are this train. What behaviours are expected, or would be considered inappropriate, by passengers on a train. For example; if it were the quiet car all passengers would expect others to be quiet and will be quiet themselves. The value here is "quiet"; it is what is valued. This value informs several behaviours:

1. We want the quiet car to remain absent of distracting noise.
2. We will challenge behaviour that does not conform to this.
3. Once in the quiet car we have a responsibility to remain quiet.

This is an example of a shared, or core, value. As can be seen; a single word, when in context has significant implications. Now, a value becomes shared when an organisation or group defines, and states, these values in a collaborative manner. It is important that these values be defined because of several factors

- Values guide each decision an individual make.

- Shared values help in setting up priorities in daily life. In a group setting, grounding these priorities in shared organisational values helps the efficacy of the organisation.
- Statements of these values helps set up what level, and type, of performance is expected of the individual as part of the group.
- Recognition, rewards, and compensation within the group will be structured to recognise those members who work according to these values.
- The group will recruit based on these values and will seek those individuals whose actions are congruent with the groups stated values.

As can be gathered, values permeate the entirety of a group identity. Be it a company, or just a collection of people; such as friends. The difference being that in a social setting people come to understand shared values through socialisation; where as a formal group does not have the liberty or luxury of doing. As such; value statements are how these desired behaviours are communicated. If one looks at the quiet example before; it is consistent with the average value statement. An effective value statement typically consists of three parts:

1. The value is given a name
2. A definition to clarify the value
3. The key behavioural expectations

For a collection of values to be effective, they will consist of usually no less than five, but not more than seven, stated values. That is to allow the values to be easily memorised. Furthermore, effective value statements are reinforceable. What is expected, and what is disallowed? If we return to our train analogy; staying quiet is expected. Thus, if someone is not quiet, what are the consequences? Being removed from the quiet car, or if the offense is great, being disallowed from continuing the journey, being the consequences in that circumstance. As such, effective value statements are reinforceable.
Now, one might be confused as to the differences between an ethics guideline, and other statements such as vision and mission statements. Below, we will explore each of these individually:

- A mission statement is what a group in fact does.
- A vision statement is what your group aspires to achieve; which can be very different from what the group currently is.
- A value statement identifies what your group considers important and essential; these values define the vision and achieve the mission.
- An ethics guide is a procedural model which guides behaviour and interactions between a provider, and vulnerable individuals and parties.

Now, ethic guidelines, and value statements do both do both focus on disallowable behaviours. However, ethical guidelines are often legally binding, and deal with behaviours considered reprehensible and potentially criminal. Value statements on the other hand deal more with actions considered inappropriate in the context of the group. There can be cross over, and often is; if we return to Module two, the BPS ethics guidelines are built specifically around four core values. However, the key difference is in the difference between values and ethics:

a. Values are the basic beliefs that an individual regard as true.
b. Ethics is guidelines or rules that are set for a society or an organisation.

As such value statements reflect the values expected of, and held by, the individual members of an organisation. Yet, ethical guidelines are explicit rules, they must be followed and do not for bend for individual morality. Though value statements may be enforceable, it is usually due to a lack of shared values, rather than actions considered unethical. For example, competitiveness may be valued in one group, or company, but may be a disadvantageous trait in a group that values mutual benefit and team work over individual successes. It is ethical, but it is against the stated values of the group.

As Jedi, the Code is our values statement. It isolates what we value, and what we expect of our fellow Jedi. If one does not meet these values, it is enforceable because of this; not following the code disallows one from being a Jedi.

If we return to where we discussed the historical, fictional codes, the mantra and creed, we can better understand why they are poor value statements:

a. The Mantra does not define its values and offers no behavioural expectations.
b. The Creed offers expectations but does not define the values behind said expectations.

Therefore, the Armonia Creed is structured in the manner it is:

1. We are Jedi; Protectors of Freedom
2. We respect our connected world
3. Thus, we serve others

The above lines state what we value: Freedom (Hence we protect it), Respect (of the world we inhabit), and Duty (We serve others).

4. By leading through example
5. By acting with integrity
6. We stay strong to support others
7. We strive for growth with our actions
8. We face adversity with wisdom and knowledge

These lines provide the behavioural expectations associated with the values stated. Not acting according to these behavioural standards makes one not a Jedi by the standard of Armonia Seminary. One can again notice over-lap with the notions of vision statements and mission statements; especially in lines 4-8, which is why it is important to distinguish. Language is flexible and adaptable; and as often works through contextual inference, as it does a literal interpretation of the words presented. Thus, the importance of quantifying the statements we make.

Assessments:

1A. Identify and define 5-7 personal values; discuss the behaviours you feel embody these values.
1B. Are these values at odds, or congruent, with a group you are active in; such as your workplace? (250 words suggested)
2A. Identify values within the Jedi Code, and define the values with arguments present in the code. Please feel free to use a code of your choice but justify said choice, otherwise, default to the Armonia Code. (5 values minimum suggested.)
2B. Are these values congruent, or at odds, with your personal values? (250 words suggested)

CAN A JEDI...

Be part of a Drone Strike or Nuclear Bomb Operation?

SCENARIO

You work for a company with a number of people who have visas to work in your country. Recently, your employer denied a renewal application of one of the visa holders ("V"). "V", of whom you have great respect for, tells you that s/he really needs the money so they can help their family back home, and asks if you would forge your employer's signature so they don't get deported.

Notes

Notes

The Jedi Code: A Jedi's True Ally?

Module Seven

Religion and the formation of Values and Ethics.

Gobekli Tepe is the oldest known human-made religious structure, and the second oldest known human made structure, and its dating places it as contemporary with the earliest agricultural developments made by man-kind. A long with early recovery of ceremonial cremations, done long before the development of human settlements. It has been part of the challenge to the once traditional narrative that religion, especially organised religion, was a later development of humanity that first required the complete development of sedentary populations made possible by agriculture. Instead; it appears that religious identities may have long been part of the human moral and ethical narrative, being part of forming group identities and thus distinct cultures.

Whether this is authentically demonstrable with further emerging discoveries is a moot point, but an interesting aside, and is part of the ongoing debate that human beings have an innate religiosity. 'The Cognition, Religion and Theology Project' (University of Oxford, 2011) which was conducted from 2008 to 2011 largely found that human beings are predisposed to believe in gods and the afterlife. Such beliefs have played an integral part in the formation of ethics and values throughout the ages; codes of ethics such as the Ten Commandments and the seven verses of Al-Fatiha are famous for adulating God and warding against the actions God finds reprehensible. Similarly; in Buddhism and Hinduism, there are the notions of "correct" or "right" thinking, speech, and action, which if adhered to shall lead to liberation from Samsara; the cycle of rebirth. This is of course a significant reductionism of the debate, but hopefully illustrates a point that religion has played a significant part in shaping both human cultures, and the ethics and values of said cultures.

A more specific example of how religion has often had a direct impact on how cultures shape themselves is to look at how they have informed the laws through the ages. For example; the Ashoka pillars and edicts, of the Emperor Asoka of the Maurya Dynasty, which are shaped by Buddhism so much as to essentially proselytise Buddhism. Many laws from Charlemagne's "Capitulatio de partibus Saxoniae" (Laws for the Saxons), are examples of Theonomy; civil laws which are derived from or dictated by Biblical law. As such they enforced Christianity upon his Saxon subjects, regardless of their faith. Similarly, Alfred the Great of the Anglo-Saxons included in his domboc (law-code) the Ten Commandments, chapters from the Book of Exodus, and the "Apostolic Letter" from the Acts of the Apostles; as such shaping his laws according to Biblical Law. To this day; several countries live under Sharia Law as dictated by the Muslim faith. Even in the west, the United Kingdom for example, there continue to be family courts which conduct themselves according to Jewish, Muslim, or other religious traditions. Though said courts have no civil power and may not dictate a punishment that goes against the law of the land; in their communities their decisions have great weight. The Amish, and other isolated religious communities may also punish their own through acts such as "shunning" if a person goes against the values of their community; a damning punishment if that individual is bereft of any other support.

As such, religion continues to affect greatly the values people live by; modern values have also been shaped by rejection or refinement of past values dictated by religion identities. An ongoing debate between elements of the religious right and secularisation in the United States is of course marriage equality. A debate that has appeared due to modern society accepting homosexuality, but those with religious sentiments rejecting this modern stance; a modern stance that was in turn a rejection of centuries old prejudices. Again, a reductionist illustration, but one that hopefully shows how religion can affect values, and how differences in values can cause conflict.

As Jedi; our code mentions the Force. In the Armonia Creed; it is explicitly said that "We are one with the Force". At first glance, this is a clear statement of spirituality. A belief that we are a part of the Force. However, the force can be both a spiritual belief, or a descriptive metaphor for a Jedi. Similarly, Jedi have varying stances on what the "Force" is, especially between those who regard it as a spiritual belief. Regardless of whether it is a statement of belief in a spiritual reality, or a metaphor for the connectedness of our actions and their consequences, it is a belief. All ethics and values are shaped by our experiences and beliefs; religion is simply the oldest vehicle by which shared values are communicated. Religious values were simply shaped by human inclinations towards Gods and the afterlife; compared to the humanist notions which shape modern ethics guides and value statements.

The Heart Sutra and the Jedi Mantra

Though neither confirmed nor denied by the original author of the Jedi Mantra, it has been noted by Jedi, and observers of the Jedi community, that the Jedi mantra bears a striking resemblance to this verse from the Heart Sutra:

1. There is no ignorance, and no end to ignorance.
2. There is no old age and death, and no end to old age and death.
3. There is no suffering, no cause of suffering, no end to suffering, no path to follow.
4. There is no attainment of wisdom, and no wisdom to attain.

One familiar with any version of the Mantra, be it the 87, 96, or 2003 version will note the similarity in language. Especially the nature of the propositional statements: "There is no ignorance, and no end to ignorance" is conceptually no different to "Ignorance, yet Knowledge". Indeed, the Jedi path has largely been influenced by Buddhism since its conception, and the works of Allan Watts are still part of the core studies of several Jedi groups. Similarly, works such as Zen in the Martial Arts were an early staple of the reading lists of many Jedi Groups. Furthermore, George Lucas has regularly talked about how his use of religious motifs in the Star Wars films, and that they were derived primarily from Christianity and Buddhism (Schell, 1999; Moyers, 1999).

Since the Jedi Praxeum in 1995 the Calming Breath Meditation, from the Buddhist practice of Anapanasati ("sati" means mindfulness; "ānāpāna" refers to inhalation and exhalation), has been a part of the Jedi tradition. The thinking and practice of Buddhism have thus been part of the Jedi Way from the inspiration to the living path. Let us consider the lesson of the entire Heart Sutra: it is a meditation on the perfection of wisdom, in which Siddhārtha Gautama recognised the five aspects of human existence, or the five aggregates of clinging, and in doing so he released himself from suffering. These five aggregates are form, sensations, feelings, mental activity, and consciousness. Conceptually, the Jedi Mantra, and the Heart Sutra do not have the same fundamental lesson, however, as discussed before in **Understanding the Mantra,** the Jedi Mantra is about freeing the self from internal conflict and developing a profound connection with reality. Both Buddhism and Jedi Philosophy expound mindfulness, and generally hold that the individual and external phenomena are both equally transient and cannot exist without one another: the necessity of mindfulness is reflected in both Sutra and Mantra.

A more thorough discussion of the parallels between the Jedi Path and Buddhism can be found in The Dharma of Star Wars (Bortolin, 2005), however, the similarity between the elements of the Heart Sutra and the Jedi Mantra should give one pause for thought on how deeply intertwined the fundamental teachings of Buddhism and the Jedi Path have been.

The Code of Chivalry

Most Jedi are from a culturally Judeo-Christian moral and ethical back-ground: being born in a largely Christion or a Post-Christian country. Places where the idealised image of the knight in shining armour has dominated folk lore about the medieval period. This has meant the Arthurian inspired notion of The Chivalric ideal has long influenced the Jedi Path. As early as 2001, Christopher Chanada, used the Code of Chivalry described by the Duke of Burgandy in the 14th century as an Inspiration for his 21 Maxims: the 21 maxims as still used in the Jedi community today.

The words the Duke of Burgendy chose to use to describe the virtues that should be shown by a Knight were as follows:

1. Faith
2. Charity
3. Justice
4. Sagacity
5. Prudence
6. Temperance
7. Resolution
8. Truth
9. Liberality
10. Diligence
11. Hope
12. Valour

The Maxims and this code have but two words in common: Faith and Justice. However, they have several synonyms, or words with very similar meanings, in common. Valour could be interpreted as courage and fearlessness is in the maxims. Temperance and Prudence satisfy the criteria of discretion from the maxims. Resolution is as suitable a word as the phrase Pure Motive as found in the maxims. Truth is the same as honesty in the maxims in this context. Diligence for the need for training and discipline outlined in the maxims.

Ultimately, little in the 21 Maxims cannot in some way be derived from the Code of Chivalry, barring the strong Eastern Influence also found in the maxims. Ultimately, the Jedi philosophy is overlaid with a code of chivalry practiced by the medieval knights of Europe. Even in the films we see the Jedi operate by a code of ethics including rules for combat, we see them abide by standards of courtesy, and hold virtues such as honour, loyalty and bravery as important and valuable. However, a key characteristic of the medieval knights was passionate attachment: loyalty to one's lord and to one's comrades-in-arms was central to both the Knightly ideal and the medieval reality. The Jedi of fiction, of course, would disavow such attachment, and indeed a theme of the Prequels was that attachment to the Republic and what it stood for undermined the Jedi Order's ability to prevent the rise of the Sith.

The path of Jedi Realism and Jediism is perhaps a middle road between the extremes: there is no harm in love, and loyalty, but attachment should not undermine morality. This is reflected in what elements of such chivalric codes survive in the Jedi Compass, be it by thematic similarly or synonyms.

Bushidō: The way of the Warrior

Many Jedi have been martial artists, and many early architects and pioneers of the Jedi path were or are Martial Artists: some amongst them professional and many other amateurs. Many have been adherents of Nihon Bujutsu (Japanese Martial Arts) or Asian disciplines. As early as the late nineties and the very start of the community, recommended reading lists produced by early leaders suggested books such as the Way of Peace by Morihei Ueshiba or the Tao of Jeet Kune Do by Bruce Lee, to give but two prominent examples.

Martial Arts creeds have been widely used by Jedi teachers to expand upon and illustrate the teachings they see as inherent to the Jedi. The Jedi Master whom identified himself by the name Mi-Zhe Fu directly quoted both the Tae Kwon Do Student Oath and the Tenets of Tae Kwon Do in his teachings:

The Student Oath of Tae Kwon Do

- I shall observe the tenets of Tae Kwon Do.
- I shall respect all instructors and seniors.
- I shall never misuse Tae Kwon Do.
- I shall be a champion of freedom and justice.
- I shall build a more peaceful world.

The Tenets of Tae Kwon Do:

- Courtesy
- Integrity
- Perseverance
- Self-control
- Indomitable spirit

Mi-Zhe Fu was not alone in this practice, and many Jedi Masters have explored their Jedi path through martial virtues and ethics. Many have used materials such as the nijū kun (Twenty Instructions) of Funakoshi Gichin or have appealed to the example of the Shaolin as ideal real-world Jedi practice. Indeed, some created original models which derived in idea from such tenets. For example, in 2007, Jesse Bendyn devised six Jedi concepts, which evidently borrow from the Tenets of Tae Kwon Do but have qualities unique to the Jedi Path:

The Jedi Concepts

1. Commitment
2. Perseverance
3. Courage
4. Leadership
5. Patience
6. Honesty

However, the warrior creed that has had the greatest influence on the Jedi Path has been that of Bushidō. The version of Bushidō which has influenced the Jedi path the most, however, is the version attributed to Nitobe Inazō. The author of Bushido: The Soul of Japan (1900), his book was one of the first major works on Bushidō written originally in English for Western readers, and as a result it has coloured the Western Concept of Bushidō. Indeed, it is still a best seller and the most widely available work in English on the topic. It is often criticized as portraying Bushidō in terms so Western as to taken away a degree of actual meaning. Inazō's eight virtues of Bushidō are often quoted by Martial Artists of a Japanese lineage, and through those active in the Jedi community they have affected the Jedi Path:

Eight virtues of Bushidō

1. Righteousness (gi)
2. Heroic Courage (yū)
3. Benevolence, Compassion (jin)
4. Respect (rei)
5. Honesty (makoto)
6. Honour (meiyo)
7. Duty and Loyalty (chūgi)
8. Self-Control (jisei)

As with the Maxims and the Compass, one can find within these virtues ideas that are evident in the terms of said Jedi documents. Duty and Loyalty, Honesty, and Respect are not readily divorced from tolerance, responsibility, and integrity. Unlike the code of chivalry, these virtues have never been used to devise a document outright, however, they have coloured people's understand of the Way of the Samurai: a way that many Jedi have used as inspiration for their path.

Assessments

1. Choose a religious code of ethics, perhaps one discussed in the lesson, and apply the "effective value statement" model from Module 3. Identify the value, define the value, and discuss the expected behaviours. (250 words suggested)
2. Is the Jedi Code a religious document? Discuss, and justify for your conclusion. Please feel free to use a code of your choice, but default to the Armonia Code if you have none. (250 words minimum)

SHOULD A JEDI....

Be a Juror or Reporting Party to a Crime which may lead to Capital Punishment?

SCENARIO

During a political campaign season, the corporation you work for reveals that they support a candidate you are vehemently against.

Notes

Notes

The Jedi Code: A Jedi's True Ally?

Module Eight

Debates in Jedi Philosophy

The Jedi code is ultimately a philosophical statement of intent; it outlines the Jedi belief structure, and what it means to be a Jedi. It is intended as a practical guide, and as such there are several underlying key debates relevant to the code.

Does Altruism exist?

An underlying question regarding the Jedi Path is that of the existence of altruism, a regular critique of being a Jedi is that no action is truly selfless. One recovers at least a psychological boon from an act of giving; for example, reinforcing a friendship, or feeling better about one self for such acts. To a Jedi this is a moot point, human beings may engage in acts which appear meaningless, but which have for that moment at least some meaning to the actor. This is true of altruistic acts, a Jedi or any individual would not engage in them if no meaning was derived from them.

However, it is important to understand these arguments to gauge a fuller comprehension of codified values. The above criticism of the Jedi path is derived from an incomplete understanding of a psychological model called the empathy-altruism hypothesis (EAH), which argues that human beings are capable of altruistic acts, but that the act of helping is always motivated by personal distress. Altruistic acts, or helping, are described as prosocial behaviours; these are behaviours or actions that benefit other people or society (Twenge et al, 2007). Personal distress is self-explanatory; anxiety, sorrow, or pain experienced by an individual in a situation.

Prosocial behaviours have largely been studied only in the context of bystander intervention; does a witness assist when they see others in distress. This skews much of the debate away from prosocial behaviour such as volunteering but it provides insight into the debate regarding altruism, and its existence. Latane and Darley (1970) created a decision model around the notion of unresponsive, and responsive bystanders. Their research suggested that a bystanders' decision to help is based on how many potential helpers they recognise as present, and that the choice to help or not is further motivated by the level of competency they believe they have. This provides an explanation for why people do not help, they perceive this help as unnecessary, and they feel they are incompetent. As Dovidio (1995) acutely notes, however, is that it is an explanation of why individuals do not help; rather than as to why they help.

A contrast, and extension to the above decision model, is the arousal-cost-reward (ACR) (Pilivian et al., 1981). It consists of the motivational part (arousal), and the cost-reward aspect which is the cognitive process of judging the cost of a helping action versus the likely outcomes. This model, and the research based upon it, have argued that the decision to help is based on several factors:

1. High-cost-for-helping/High-cost-for-not-helping dilemma:
What is the relative cost of either out come? Is the cost of helping, or not helping, too great?

2. Redefining the situation:
Can the situation be revised to a point where help is necessary or unnecessary?

3. Diffusing responsibility:
Are there other, more capable, potential helpers at hand? Is there someone else at hand to take responsibility?

4. Victim blaming:
Can the situation be defined to blame the victim for their own misfortune? Would helping be inappropriate because of sentiments about the victim.

Beside the factors above; in this model it was also found that the type of help needed, victim characteristics, and bystander gender were a factor. Pilivian et al (1969) showed these factors in his observational study; where student experimenters pretended to be either disabled (Lame) or drunk. They faked a collapse in a subway, and 90 percent of bystanders would assist the Lame experimenter, compared to 20 percent whom would help the drunk experimenter. The justification made by these bystanders being that the drunk had brought the situation upon himself. The drunk experimenter did not act belligerent or aggressive; which could be a factor in a person choosing to not try and help. However, a fall victim can be a time intensive helping situation; which can explain why several bystanders did not aid the Lame experimenter either. Again, this model offers many explanations as to why people help but leaves questions unanswered.

At this point we can return to the empathy-altruism hypothesis. This model specifically defines altruism specifically as the motivation for our actions to help the recipient of our help. As mentioned, in short, the EAH argues that human beings are capable of altruistic acts, but that the act of helping is always motivated by personal distress. This is related the negative state relief (NSR) model; which argues that humans help others purely to reduce their own distress at seeing others in need of help. However; Dovidio and Penner (2004) in a meta-analysis of 20 years of study on the EAH model argued thus; "truly altruistic motivation may exist and all helping is not necessarily egotistically motivated". Indeed, this is supported by Batson et al (1991) whom reported that participants who reported high levels of empathetic concern displayed high levels of helping regardless of whether they experienced empathic joy from helping. These individuals did not reduce their distress by helping, nor did they receive any egotistical benefit.

To return to the key question, does altruism exist? In short, the debate is ongoing. There are acts of altruism the traditional models cannot explain, for example, the heroic acts of many people during emergencies to help those they have no connection to. To again quote Dovidio and Penner (2004); "Helping is a complex multidimensional behaviour".

To the Jedi, whether altruism exists is a moot point. We do not care if helping actions are in any manner egotistical, so long as our actions are for the benefit of those we look to help. We do not expect reward or recognition, but we do find meaning in our path by putting the needs of others before our own when called to do so. Whatever psychological benefit we derive from helping others does not matter; it does not undo or cheapen what good we do in the world.
Hopefully, this greater discussion on psychological altruism has also illustrated why Jedi do not engage in Comtean Altruism. If altruism is in any manner egotistically driven; the moment, we act according to beliefs that we know what is best for others, we are potentially serving only our own concept of "good". We are creating an environment in which we need not experience distress, but in doing so we devalue the right of others to make their own decisions. Though we might consider the decisions of others unwise, so long as it harms no other, or has no legal implications, we have no right to force our notion of help upon them.

Moral Realism and Relativism?

Moral, or ethical, realism posits that statements about ethics refer to objective features of reality; and that they may be correct to varying degrees. In short, moral realism holds that there are moral facts that are objectively known, or can be known, and they are objective in that they exist independently of human attitudes. This contrasts with what is known as meta-ethical moral relativism, which posits that objective morality does not exist; that there are no moral facts.

An advantage of moral realism is that it can resolve moral disagreements: If moral beliefs contradict one another, realism says that they cannot all be correct, and therefore one belief must be right and another wrong. Contrast this with normative moral relativism, that argues that nobody is right or wrong from an objective stance, we are obligated to tolerate the behaviour of others even when we disagree about the morality of their behaviours. However, not all moral relativists hold this normative position: some argue that just because morals are relative it does not make all beliefs equally valid.

Humanity functionally practices both as societies; the laws of the land are a form of moral realism. Something is either objectively legal or illegal. Social groups form because of shared values, and behaviours; a non-conforming behaviour is objectively "wrong" to said social group. However, in larger society, we nominally accept and tolerate the reality that not every-one believes as we do. Similarly, even close-knit social groups may have values dissonance between some members, and yet these differences are tolerated.

As Jedi, we practice moral realism as a sub-culture. There is a Jedi way to be, and a non-Jedi way to be. Something is either Jedi-like, or not Jedi-like, and we resolve our internal politics based on this moral reality. However, we accept the right of non-Jedi to live as they like; they are not part of our sub-culture. We accept moral relativism to the extent that we accept there are moral behaviours we do not agree with, but we cannot argue as being objectively wrong.

The path of the Jedi is one that is Deontological in nature: an action itself is right or wrong according to the Jedi Code; it outlines what is Jedi like behaviour, and by implied exclusivity tells us what is not. When helping others we seek to aid through consent always, and to give as much freedom where possible for people to be helped as they desire. We understand that people may want to be helped in a manner that we might not want for ourselves; and unless it is illegal, may cause undue distress, or goes against an ethical guide you are beholden to, ultimately it is part our duty as Jedi to help.

I have mentioned consent, and mentioned why we would not help someone, but I would like to go on a short aside. If you find someone unconscious, and their life is in-danger, to help them to preserve their life even without their explicit consent is the correct course of action if you can do it safely. This is an extreme example, but not entirely unlikely, if someone is a volunteer or works in a relatively dangerous environment. We look to help with consent; but in the event someone cannot give it, and they are unconscious, we can assume they would probably want us to save their life or do our best to do so.

Utilitarianism and Jedi

Utilitarianism prescribes acts that maximize good consequences for all of society; the needs of the many outweigh those of the few, or of the one. One might believe Jedi to be utilitarianism, but this would be inaccurate. An issue with Utilitarianism, as with Comtean Altruism, is that its fundamental principle ignores key factors. The good of the many can come at the expense of the few, and in unjust ways. Hitler and the National Socialist Party had success in restoring past-war Germany's economy; what they did was for the good of much of the German population. However, it was at the expense of the Jewish community, the disabled, of political rivals, and of the rights of women. There is no logical justification for why theft, and outright denigration, should be acceptable means of helping the masses.

Now; let us be clear, that is a strawman example, and no utilitarian worth their salt would argue that the methods of the Nazi party to restore Germany's Economy were justifiable. However, it does reflect the danger of the basic algorithm of act in the way that helps the most people. Someone must bear the burden, and the cost, and the question must be asked; is it fair? As Jedi, we do hope that our actions will reach and help the most people in our community as possible; but we must never act in a way that sees the burden meted out unfairly. From this notion; Jedi act from the perspective of Effective Value-Based altruism. Jedi apply evidence and reason to determine the most effective ways our actions may help others. A Jedi is to consider actions, and potential outcomes, and act according to predicted greatest positive outcome. We do all this while considering our values; fairness, freedom, autonomy, and individual growth. We accept that costs are gained, but we do not abandon our values in the face of a challenge; the end does not justify the means. All means create their own ends, and unfair, and unjust means, will in time bring unfair and unjust ends. The greater goal does not eclipse the here and now.

Final Thoughts

The above three debates, and notions underline the Jedi Code, and Jedi Ethos, but they are not the lone debates that occur about the Jedi Path. We have only briefly touched on very sophisticated topics, and I would encourage you the reader to study each of these topics further. Hopefully, this section has offered answers to what I hope to have been emerging thoughts, and queries, about the Jedi Code and its use in life.

ASSIGNMENT:

Choose one of the three debates discussed in this Module, and explore the discussion online (either through personal research or with others around you/in the forums). After reviewing the information, how do you feel what you have learned relates to the Jedi Code?

SHOULD A JEDI...

Conduct Animal Testing for Medicinal Purposes?

SCENARIO

While on social media, you notice a discussion occurring between friends, about topic you have a lot of knowledge and passion for. Unfortunately, the discussion has taken a turn for the worst, and many people look upset.

Notes

The Jedi Code: A Jedi's True Ally?

Module Nine

The Code & The Compass

Just as an exercise, go to Wookieepedia and look up "The Jedi Code". At the top of the article are two tabs, one reads "Canon" and the other reads "Legends". Go ahead and click on the Legends and look for the heading "Following the Jedi Code".

Looking over the tenets underneath, does it look familiar to you? If not, let's do another experiment- pull up the Jedi Compass.

Now do you see it?

What is on Wookieepedia is called "The Jedi Behaviors", and these were used by the Jedi Community early on. Eventually the Jedi Community wanted to have more appropriate tenets to follow, after all "Duty to the Republic" doesn't exactly work for a world-wide belief system. From this endeavor to find more relevant tenets, the community got pieces such as The Jedi Jewels, The 21 Maxims of Jediism, and the 33 Jedi Teachings (which is often used in it's shorter version of 16 Teachings). For some of these pieces, there have been alterations from order to order to better clarify what each tenet should mean to the Jedi Path. But of all these, the Jedi Compass may be the closest resemblance to the fictional Jedi Behaviors. And that's not by accident, the first document used to figure out what is and isn't part of the Real Life Jedi Path, was the Jedi Behaviors. Then going line by line of each popular document, things were crossed out or reworded until finally the Jedi Pyramid was developed and taken from order to order until it was edited to be something the whole community agreed with. For whatever it was worth, somehow the new document, now called the Jedi Compass, maintained a lot of recognizable speech. "Honor the Law", became "Respect the Law"; "Duty to the Republic" became "Duty to All"; and "Conquer Recklessness" became "Overcome Recklessness", just as examples.

In the fiction, the Jedi Code itself wasn't exactly enough to help a Jedi figure out their way in the world. So the Behaviors were established to inform one on how to live by the Jedi Code. In this way, one could not easily pervert a line of the Jedi Code and maintain innocence that the Jedi Path led them to believe they were doing the right thing.

ASSIGNMENT

For your assignment, look at each tenet of the Jedi Compass and explain how the Jedi Code supports it.

Assignment

1) Turn in your final paper.

SHOULD A JEDI...

Administer Euthenasia

SCENARIO

You are a knight in an offline Jedi Chapter. You are currently unmarried and you do not have children. While serving as a knight you take on an apprentice, whom you learn later on during the apprenticeship has romantic feelings for you.

Notes

The Jedi Code: A Jedi's True Ally?

Extra Credit Assignments

My Values Aren't the Values of the Jedi Code....

Maybe they aren't. But there is one more question that we, as Jedi, should ask: Does the Jedi Code's values prevent us from exercising our own values? Let's go back to the Abortion example.

If you found that the Jedi Code affords you the right to an abortion, then is there really anything stopping you from not having an abortion?

But maybe that's not the reason it causes you concern. A key component missing in the discussion about abortion in the United States is the "WHY" Christianity feels threatened by things like homosexuality or abortion. For many of them, God's Wrath could be right around the corner, and they don't want to catch it themselves. To them, they are modern representations of the prophets which tried to tell Israel they were in for it if they didn't stop sinning.

To really determine if the Jedi Path is for you, you need to put everything into prospective and make a decision on whether or not you truly the follow the Jedi Code.

Which is another facet to the whole conversation- what trumps what? That's what the next few page in this study are dedicated to help you determine. This section isn't part of the certification process, it's for you to contemplate the way forward.

Try another Jedi Code

Sometimes, to understand something, we have to look at things which were inspired by the source material. During this course, you've been exposed to other Jedi Codes- choose one that you didn't use and try analyzing the main character in 5 episodes of a television show you really enjoy against the new code.

Television Show: _____

Episode Name: _____

Television Show: _____

Episode Name: _____

Television Show: _____

Episode Name: _____

Television Show: _____

Episode Name: _____

Television Show: _____

Episode Name: _____

Comparison

Now that you have had some time to analyze another code, how does the previous Jedi Code measure up? And how do you feel about the Jedi Code as a whole?

The Force or the Jedi Code?

There is an argument in the Jedi Community about what makes a Jedi. There are those which believe a Jedi follows the Force, and then there are those which believe it's the Jedi Path that makes you a Jedi. Armonia contends that following the Force does not qualify you as a Jedi. We also contend that belief in the Force is not enough to be a Jedi. And here's 2 reasons why:

1) In the Star Wars Universe there were many groups which believed in the Force, the most noteworthy being the Sith. Thus, if the only thing needed to be a Jedi is to believe in the Force, the Sith would thus be Jedi. But what separated the Sith and Jedi from one another was philosophical differences.

2) As much as people can hate on the Prequels and the Sequels, there is one philosophical take away that has value: there were disagreements about what the "Will of the Force" is. Qui-Gon Jinn believed that the Force led him to Anakin to restore balance in the Force. But the Council wasn't so certain.

    Even in the Original Trilogy, Yoda suggested there was no one person that would restore balance, but rather that the Force will find it's own way to accommodate it. Speculation is that Yoda referred to Leia. But even Leia might not have succeeded.

    And then, in the Sequels, Rey learns swiftly that the Force has opposing wills. One that is of the Light, and one that is of the Dark. These forces seem to be in a constant struggle to win out against one another.

    Ultimately, we can see that man's fallibility to determine the "Will of the Force" creates a major problem in following it.

An argument i see to counter these things, is that the Jedi Path was written after the Will of the Light Side of the Force. In truth, this fails a test as well. To believe such is to believe that the author of a Role-Playing Game in the 1980s, and subsequently those of us in the Jedi Community which have developed the Jedi Path for a real world system knew the Will of the Force. But let's be honest, the guy RPG book was written for a fictional universe. It was creatively put together, and tried to instill modern morals and values into the fiction. We, the Community, believed it could be adapted for the real world- and what we have put together is what we believe can move us forward into an ethical, moral and healthy lifestyle benefitting all around us.

That's not the Force, that's philosophy of what we believe represents "Light" today. Furthermore, no one who has written these pieces has claimed to be in direct contact with the Force to obtain this wisdom.

So what is it that trumps what? For a Jedi, the Jedi Code is what keeps us in check. It can be there to prevent us from doing something unethical, even when we hear that small voice trying to convince us that what we are doing is the will of some supernatural force trying to move humanity along it's path. For us, we can refer back to the Jedi Code and ask "But is this what I believe is the right thing?"

So ask yourself- Are you willing to take a chance in bearing loyalty to the Force? Or will you remain loyal to the Jedi Code?

Notes

Notes

The Jedi Compass
By The Jedi Community

The Ineffable

The Force- "The Force" is a loosely adapted term to explain a something which all cultures agree exist, but disagree on exactly what it is. As such, a Jedi dedicates themselves to understanding of all things within and through "the Force". As a rule, no Jedi can set down in law a concrete definition of "the Force" for all to follow, only for themselves.

Core Ethics

Loyalty to the Jedi Code- This has a few different variants depending on what order a Jedi attends. A Jedi is bound by the code. By maintaining your loyalty to the code, you are able to keep your actions in check through the moral integrity of the Jedi Path outlined in the Jedi Code. It is important that a Jedi checks their own version of the code against the original codes (Jedi Code and Skywalker Code) before they adopt it.

Duty to the All- A Jedi's mission is to support their community through service. A Jedi is charged with acting, objectively, when they recognise a situation where someone needs help. Jedi put their lives above the lives of others, even when facing danger, but know that they can help through direct action or indirect action as per the situation.

Respect the Law- A Jedi knows enough of the law to operate within it. Jedi should respect, and do their best to live by, the laws of the land they are living in. However, these are man's law, and like man, subject to flaws. A Jedi must act for the best interest of mankind as he/she sees the situation.

Defense- A Jedi understands that defense is not purely physical, but that there are many ways to defend a person or property. As such, it is important to understand that Jedi are not vigilantes. If, however, they are in a position where they are called to defend themselves or someone else against loss of life, limb or eyesight, they are allowed to apply the appropriate amount of force necessary for defense.

Action- A Jedi recognizes that there are times when getting involved with a situation is against the will of the person they are seeking to assist, or that helping them may be more detrimental in the long run. As such, a Jedi seeks inner wisdom to determine when to act and when not to act.

Self Awareness

Interior- A Jedi works to become aware of their emotions and things which make them "tick". They learn of their flaws and strengths, seeking to reconcile a life with those flaws which they cannot change and the strengths they have been blessed with. In this a Jedi must be constantly looking inward for their motivations, their directions, what moves them, and why they allow it to do so.

Exterior- It is important that a Jedi be aware of the person they present to those around them, and how that will affect the dynamic of the groups they find themselves in. How one's presence is received will determine whether or not the next steps will be met with hostility or acceptance.

Virtues

Tolerance- You do not need to agree with someone's religion, their nationality, their career choice, their dress or anything else for that matter. Tolerance is not about agreement, it is about showing respect for the freedom of a persons choices and to respect their choices, until it reaches a point in which a reasonable person would consider the individual's actions as a/an (emotionally, spiritually, financially, and/or physically) abusive threat to you or another person.

Responsibility- Responsibility is at the heart of learning to overcome our problems. A Jedi should be held responsible for all of their actions. Without it, we cannot grow, we cannot help others and we cannot justify why we are to be taken seriously.

Discipline- In order to walk the Jedi Path, you need to live by your training and by the philosophy. It is your responsibility to continue your growth throughout the rest of your life. Even while you are training with a mentor or taking a course at an order, it is discipline that will get you through to your knighthood and beyond.

Fortitude- Fortitude is the emotional strength and conviction to press forward in any given situation which poses an internal or external adversity. Developing fortitude allows a Jedi to show that they are not willing to give up until they have drawn their last breath.

Integrity- A Jedi seeks to maintain their integrity to the Jedi Code at all times. A Jedi should hold themselves to a high standard knowing that what they do when no one is looking is just as important as what they do when people are looking.

Objectivity- A Jedi trains themselves to gain as much relevant information as possible before drawing their conclusions. Once intelligence has been collected, they approach the problem with as little cultural and emotional bias as possible so that they are able to develop a decision on their next action.

Overcome

Aggression- To build on the Jedi Virtues, a Jedi must keep themselves open to the world. Through the misuse of aggression, they miss out on opportunities to further their cause. This does not preclude being assertive. A Jedi needs to learn to find the most effective means of resolving a conflict through the least bit of hostility possible.

Recklessness- A Jedi does not take unnecessary risks, knowing that their life is important to the Jedi Mission of bettering the world around them. In overcoming recklessness, a Jedi acknowledges and is mindful of how small the impact is perceived to have on themselves or others.

Attachments- Overcoming your attachments is not about getting rid of all your possessions or even denouncing your family, instead this is about forward movement. In overcoming/subjagating your attachments, you are acknowledging what value these things have to you, and you recognize that there comes a time when you should no longer fight for your attachments, and you must let go. For a Jedi overcoming attachments can extend to bad habits, unhealthy obsessions, and connections to people that make us less who we have chosen to be.

Prowess

Defense Art - A "Defense Art" is not necessarily physical in nature, it can be through speech, writing, diplomacy, art or a number of other options which lead to an active method of curing the world of oppression. Like many of the other disciplines, you may find that your Defense Art is the same as another art (Physical, Scholarly, or Spiritual).

Physical Art - A Jedi should seek a physical art within their capabilities which keeps them them in shape and focuses on maintaining discipline of their body. . Part of the physical art, which can be observed by all Jedi regardless of their mobility, is health. A Jedi should eat right, and maintain their health to the best of their ability.

Scholarly Art - A Jedi should seek out skills that provide benefit to them and the people around them. The search for knowledge is fundamental to Jedi as one never stops learning, seeking knowledge or bettering their skills.

Spiritual Art - A spiritual art may be as simple as developing meditation, but can go far beyond this. A Jedi may choose to develop a spiritual art aimed at connecting them with "the Force" through healing, seeking guidance, or simply developing their own self awareness.

CITATIONS

Batson, C. D., & Shaw, L. L. (1991). Evidence for altruism: Toward a pluralism of prosocial motives. Psychological Inquiry, 2, 107-122.

Bendyn, J (2008) Teachings. Retrieved from http://tenebraesurgunt.angelfire.com/info.html. Accessed February 13, 2019.

Chanada, C. (2001) The 21 Maxims. Jediism: The Jedi Religion. Retrieved from https://web.archive.org/web/20020311131535/http://www.jediism.org. Accessed February 13, 2019.

Cramer, P. (2006). Protecting the Self. The Guilford Press. p. 17. ISBN 9781593855284.

Dovidio JF, Penner LA. 2001. Helping and altruism. In International Handbook of Social Psychology: Interpersonal Processes, ed. G Fletcher, M Clark, pp. 162–95. Oxford: Blackwell Sci.

Dovidio, J. F. (1995). Helping behavior. In A. S. R. Manstead & M. Hewstone (Eds.), Blackwell encyclopedia of social psychology. Oxford: Basil Blackwell. Gyatso, T. (2005) Essence of the Heart Sutra. Wisdom Publications.

Inazō, N. (2002) Bushido: The Soul of Japan. Kodansha International, Tokyo. Kidohdin. (2009) The 22 Jedi Teachings at Jedi Sanctuary. The Jedi Sanctuary. Recovered from: https://web.archive.org/web/20090227102448/http://www.jedisanctuary.org/pages/teachings/teachings-from-starwars.htm. Accessed February 13, 2019.

Latane´, B., & Darley, J. M. (1970). The unresponsive bystander: Why doesn't he help? New York, NY: Appleton-Century-Croft.

Legislation.gov.uk. (2010). Equality Act 2010. [online] Available at: http://www.legislation.gov.uk/ukpga/2010/15/contents [Accessed 2018, February 6].

Moyers, B. (1999) Of Myth and Man: A conversation between Bill Moyers and George Lucas about the meaning of the Force and the true theology of Star Wars. Time.
Piliavin, I.M., Rodin, J.A. & Piliavin, J. (1969) Good Samaritanism: An underground phenomenon? Journal of Personality and Social Psychology, 13, 289 -99)

Piliavin, J. A., Dovidio, J. F., Gaertner, S. L., & Clark, R. D. III (1981). Emergency intervention. New York: Academic Press.

Schell, O. (1999) I'm the Cynic who has hope for the Human Race. New York Times.

Tedeschi, M. (2003). Taekwondo: Traditions, Philosophy, Technique. Weatherhill, Inc.

The Baronage Press and Pegasus Associates Ltd (1999) Chivalry. Retrieved from https://www.baronage.co.uk/chivalry/chival1a.html. Accessed February 13, 2019.

Twenge, J. M., Zhang, L., Catanese, K. R., Dolan-Pascoe, B., Lyche, L. F., & Baumeister, R. F. (2007). Replenishing connectedness: Reminders of social activity reduce aggression after social exclusion. British Journal of Social Psychology, 46, 205–224.

University of Oxford. (2011). Humans 'predisposed' to believe in gods and the afterlife. ScienceDaily. Retrieved August 8, 2018 from www.sciencedaily.com/releases/2011/07/110714103828.htm

Printed in Great Britain
by Amazon